The People's Hi

Blyth
Then And Now

by

Constance Atkinson, Peter Butters,
David Durward and Eldred Routledge

Blyth Civic Centre, formerly the Cowpen & Crofton Colliery Welfare Institute –
opened in 1926.

Previous page: The Pit Wheel, sited in the grounds of Blyth Civic Centre to
commemorate the mining industry.

First published in 1999 by

The People's History Ltd
Suite 1
Byron House
Seaham Grange Business Park
Seaham
Co. Durham
SR7 0PY

ISBN 1 902527 44 5

Contents

Aerial view showing Broadway Circle under construction in 1931. In the distance, the miner's houses of Cowpen Colliery (West, Double, Gas, New and Badger Rows) are visible in the left hand corner. The two distinct buildings are the Miners' Welfare (left) and Dinsdale House surrounded by farm land, market gardens and small allotments.

Aerial photograph of the mineral line leading from the staithes to the station passing between the Gas Works and the Dry Docks, *circa* 1930.

Introduction

Looking back into the past is something we all do from time to time. The words 'Do you remember?' can be induced by meeting an old friend or looking at an old photograph. A great deal of nostalgia may unfold when we reflect on the changes that have taken place between 'Then' and 'Now'. By putting together a collection of comparative photographs from different generations in this book, I believe the authors have catered for a range of readers. Those who wish to look back directly into the past are encouraged to do so, but the collection should also appeal to some younger readers. For by looking at two photographs taken from the same spot at different periods in time they can question when and why did the changes take place

The growing interest in the past is evident today from the number of people researching family history. They will spend hours looking at microfilms and microfiche of census returns, parish records and the International Genealogical Index. As the knowledge of their family grows, the desire for even more detailed information increases, and some will travel long distances to find locations where their ancestors once lived. For them, just one picture of a place or person directly linked to their family can be looked upon as a great find. Perhaps one of the photographs in this book may provide such a reward.

My most graphic memory of the past in Blyth must be centred around the rows of miners' houses at Cowpen Colliery where my grandfather lived for over fifty years. I can still clearly remember the miners trudging home at the end of the shift at Crofton Mill Pit, still wearing knee pads and headgear, with their faces and work clothes covered in black dust. This was before the days of pithead baths and with no bathroom or running water in the house, instead the tin bath would be ready in front of the fire of the black leaded kitchen range. Although there was a shared water tap across the row, water was often drawn from the rain butt in the yard and heated in huge pans and kettles on the fire. Many were the times that I was firmly told to wash in a basin of that cold water before sitting down for a meal. Just off the kitchen was a spotlessly clean, but icy cold, pantry with whitewashed walls and a wooden bench scrubbed almost white. Secure in the comforts of today, I am full of admiration for the way families coped then in such spartan conditions. Probably sanitation was the most difficult aspect with the outside toilet being a circular hole cut in the wooden planks. Again the walls were whitewashed and I remember the difficult high step and the squares of newspaper on a string hanging from a large nail. Every few days a team of men equipped with shovels and a holding tank had the unpleasant task of cleaning out from the trapdoor at the back.

The miners were proud men and truly reflected the town's motto 'We grow by industry'. In the early 1950s, three and a half thousand worked underground and on the surface of the five mines within the borough. Outputs increased and by 1961, with additional coal from other pits in Northumberland, Blyth became the largest coal shipping port in Europe.

The beach was a popular venue for relaxation for the miners and their families. Children and parents playing and picnicking together and a myriad of box-like green tents. On one day in the mid 1950s the council actually hired out two hundred and sixty of these tents and one and a half thousand deckchairs. Of course, the picnic would not be complete without a pot of tea, the hot water obtained from the hatch at the side of the Jubilee Cafe. Today these facilities are not available and of course people have a greater variety of recreations available to them. In the 1960s, the view from the beach out to sea always seemed to have something to catch the eye, with seventy ships a week carrying coal to distant ports, fishing boats going to and fro and occasionally the appearance of one of the larger vessels built in Blyth undertaking sea trials.

Many people will recall the devastation felt when the news broke in 1966 that the Blyth Shipyard was to close. A great tradition going back to the beginning of the nineteenth century was over but important ships like the *Ark Royal* in 1914 and the *Pacific Princess* fifty years later should not be forgotten. The building slipways were large enough for a 20,000 ton ship and when near completion such a vessel would vastly overshadow the houses along Regent Street. Another feature of the time, I recall, occurred each day when the shipyard workers finished their work. Like a sudden explosion the bicycles would pour out of the yard gate and sweep through the centre of the town.

The town centre buildings have undergone many changes even in the last half century. The railway station, two cinemas, a large theatre and six prominent churches have all been demolished. The role of the churches and their contribution to the spiritual and social life of the town over the years has been vital to its development. Their part was well recorded week by week in the pages of the town's newspaper, the *Blyth News*, and even that has gone now. Of the major buildings remaining the churches are the oldest – St Wilfrid's (built in 1861), St Mary's (1864) and United Reform (1876).

A few of our other buildings have date stones although in the rush of life today we often fail to look upwards to see them and be aware of the attractive architectural features. Some brick buildings, the Library (1882), the Police Station (1896) and Barclays Bank show that with good maintenance they do stand the test of time. The facade of Lloyds Bank demonstrates that large expanses of plate glass are not necessary to modern business today. However, it is unfortunate when the character of a street is spoilt by the intrusion of a modern, styless building – Bridge House in Bridge Street being the obvious example. Next door the new office development under construction does appear to have more in keeping with the original buildings. Opposite the bus station stands the old Hedley Young's building. This once took pride of place amongst all the town's shops, but now through neglect the fabric is deteriorating rapidly and with painted black windows will do nothing to attract visitors to our town.

Some readers on looking through this collection will realise that they have a photograph in an album or a box at home showing some aspect of life in the history of Blyth. They perhaps may not realise that they are in fact local historians and I would urge them to secure any old photographs for posterity by loaning them to the authors or to the Local History Society. This book, by the very use of 'Then' and 'Now' photographs is a form of 'time capsule' for the new Millennium, not to be stored away to be discovered later but to be available and enjoyed by all now.

Peter Butters
Blyth, 1999

AROUND THE TOWN

ARP Wardens marching along Regent Street during the Victory Parade in 1945. The gentleman on the right of the front row is Mr W.R. Sullivan and beside him is Mr W. Middleton.

When this photograph was taken after the First World War, Regent Street was the hub of Cowpen Quay. Running North to South from Hodgeson's Road to the railway bridge leading to the railway station and then from the bridge down to Bridge Street, which was called Turner Street, but both now form part of Regent Street.

Regent Street had its own church, Regent Street Primitive Methodist Church, built in 1899. There were three public houses, The Croft, The Buffalo and the Traveller's Rest. There was also a multitude of shops (Authors' note – we apologise if we have missed anyone out.), which have changed hands over the years, including:

Fordyce the chemist; Smith's pie shop which became a bakery belonging to Jack Gilbertson; Marshall's bakery; Bullen the cobbler; John Mather's Post Office and newsagents; Gallon's music shop; Gleghorn and Cole the barbers; Seghini's Ice Cream Parlour; Diamondstone the jeweller; Dunn's the stationer's; Joseph Lee's; David Gillis furniture; Arkles and Cooknell's drapers; Miss Dover renowned for her millinery; Alfie Boast and Stokers were men's outfitters. The Co-Operative Society had several branches including their tailor's shop.

The stationery chain T&G Allen traded in the street for several years. Miss Mary's was a popular confectioner as was the Supreme Sweet Shop. A shop just under the railway bridge (now demolished) was Turnbull's the tobacconist.

Tommy Henderson was the owner of the first fish and chip shop in the area followed by William's and then Martin's respectively.

At least four grocers, the Co-Op, Walter Willson's, Gallon's and Thompson's Red Stamps Stores flourished. There were also butchers shops owned by Arthur Fail, Alf Shy, William Redford, Taits, Atkinson and Hindhaugh, Mark McKay, Thomas Yorke and Jack Hill, Greengrocery was supplied by Thompson's and Armstrong's. The oldest established trader in Blyth still has his original shop in Regent Street, John Herron the jeweller.

Regent Street was famous for its stampede. This happened when the shipyard buzzer sounded at 12 noon and again at five o'clock, when over one thousand men and boys poured into the street from the shipyard, some on bikes, some running and some walking, but all heading home for lunch or tea.

Today, Regent Street is a sad reflection of what it was. The church has gone, as have most of the shops, with the exception of John Herron's the jewellers. The Croft pub is now called Joe Cavner's after previously being named the Porthole. The Buffalo is now a community centre and the Traveller's Rest has been demolished. The shipyard and railway station were closed in the 1960s.

Plessey Road, *circa* 1900. On the corner of Ridley Street were Alder's the compass adjusters. In 1963 Tommy Nicholson built a garage on this site for his nephew Joe Nicholson. The business was named the Blyth Motor Company. The garage was closed in 1994 and part of it was demolished and the Quayside Court housing complex (pictured below) was built on the site. The garage workshops are still standing, unfortunately vandalised.

The Boer War memorial in Blyth erected shortly after the end of the conflict. It stood at the junction of Blagdon Street and Bridge Street. It was moved to the Cenotaph in Ridley Park when that was erected after the Second World War.

The site today. The shops have changed hands many times. They are now occupied by a painter and decorator and an Insurance Broker, the shops were previously occupied by Thread's Bridal Hire, Thirlwell's DIY, Northern Builders and William Horn, an undertaker and builder. As can be seen in the top photograph, the building had previously been the Blyth Pharmacy and the town's Post Office.

Bridge Street, pre 1914. The shops on the left hand side of the photograph are Charlie Thompson's pie shop, Miss Kelsey's fruit and vegetable shop, Ross the jeweller, Dolan's the bakers, Parson's estate agents, Dixon Wilson the butcher and Dalston's the ironmonger. The large building beyond the shops was the English Presbyterian Church. Bridge House now occupies the site. Shipowners, captains and a vice consul lived in the houses on the right.

The Arriva garage (previously United) now occupies the site. Since this photograph was taken in August 1998, the two blocks of shops on the left have been demolished, leaving only Julietta's Pizzeria Restaurant standing. An office block replacing the shops.

Two views of the Renwick Road, Waterloo Road junction. The photograph above shows the junction as it was prior to the houses on both sides of Waterloo Road being demolished to make way for the proposed dual carriageway which never came to fruition. The bottom photograph shows the junction today with the mini-roundabout replacing the cross roads. Sidney Street was blocked off when the mini-roundabout was constructed.

Bath Terrace in the 1930s. It was formerly known as Paradise Row and Shiney Row and received its present name when the Baths were constructed. This photograph shows some of the oldest houses in Blyth. The centre block on the right was built in the eighteenth century – the exact date is not known as the deeds to the properties were lost in a fire at Blagdon Hall. Beyond the houses on the right is the old St Cuthbert's vicarage that is now the site of the Kingdom Hall of Jehovah's Witnesses built in 1997. On the left is the Ridley Arms built in 1788 originally as a private house for shipowner and rope maker George Marshall. It became a public house in the early nineteenth century. However, it fell into disrepair and was demolished to make way for new housing in 1968 despite it being a listed building.

Bath Terrace today. Missing is the police station chimney dominating the skyline. It was demolished in the early 1960s after it was found that it was in a state of decay. This coincided with the change over from coal to gas heating in the police station. After the chimney was demolished the police received several letters from shipping companies asking why the chimney was demolished as it was used as a navigation landmark.

The Ropery and Ridley Avenue. In the centre are the long low buildings of the Rope Walks. As the name suggests, this was where ropes of all descriptions were made, many going to the ships that used the river. The building in the foreground is now the site of Ridley Avenue, and the one in the background is Park View. The large building on the left was the Ridley Arms. The row of terraced houses behind the 'Ridley' is Bath Terrace.

In this photograph, taken approximately 100 years later, the roofs of the houses in Wellington Street can be seen in the foreground. Foster Street, Ridley Avenue and the south side of Bath Terrace also appear. The wind farm generators on the North Pier are also visible, they were erected in 1992. Also in the photograph is the new Kingdom Hall (far left centre). The photographs on this page were both taken from the roof of St Cuthbert's Church Tower as were the next two.

Some of the shops in Market Street, now part of Plessey Road. The building on the right was the King's Head Hotel. The name was changed in recent years to 'Jumpin Jax' and more recently to 'Durty Nelly's' Irish Bar. The scaffolding poles in the foreground mark the start of the building of the police station in Northumberland Street around 1894-96. The tops of the south side coal staithes can be seen in the background with a train of wagons on top. The masts of ships being loaded can be seen just beyond.

This photograph, taken in August 1998, shows the vast changes that have taken place. The rear of the police station dominates the area. The bins of the Alcan jetty can be seen on the skyline. The office blocks of Sextant House and Compass House can be seen on the left, these were built during 1991-92 in Freehold Street.

Newsham Road Railway Bridge, 1967. This was one of three bridges which crossed the roads of Blyth. Each being the dividing line between two streets. This bridge separated Princess Louise Road from Newsham Road. The other two bridges were between Turner Street and Regent, and Belgrave Crescent and Wensleydale Terrace. It was said at this time, 'There is no way in or out of Blyth unless you pass over or under a railway line.'

The scene in 1999. The Leisure Centre can be seen through the trees.

Cowpen Central Workshops (N.C.B.) in 1956, better known as the 'Colliery Yard'. Before nationalisation in 1947 the yard was controlled by the Cowpen Coal Company who owned the coal mines in the area. It was first established in 1797 when the first mine, the South Pit, was sunk and was only a matter of yards from the pithead. In those early days, the skilled men required would be mainly blacksmiths and joiners.

Tom Morgan, a blacksmith, standing in front of the Blacksmith's Shop in the Colliery Yard in the early 1950s. The shop had two forge hammers and several furnaces. In front of the Blacksmith's Shop are two pithead cages for transporting men and coal tubs to and from the surface, axles and wheels for the tubs and a framework for a main tunnel. The smaller building on the right was the Pay Office.

Cowpen Road. The gable end of the building on the extreme left of both photographs was, and is, the King's Arms on Cowpen Road. The cottages have been replaced with a garage built for Blyth Co-Operative Society. The garage is now occupied by Blyth Valley Ford.

Cowpen Road looking east towards Blyth, 1900. This tranquil scene with the cattle strolling down the middle of the road is a far cry from the Cowpen Road of today. The houses on the left were demolished before the Second World War and in 1938 the Council built a small estate on the site.

Today the road has been straightened and made wider. Traffic lights and a mini-roundabout give easier access to Cowpen Industrial Estate and Cowpen housing estate. The Bebside and Horton Schools were built on the opposite side of the road. The photograph was taken from the lay-by of the Kitty Brewster pub (formerly the Foresters Arms). Built before 1873, the name was changed in 1976.

The Catholic School at Cowpen in the 1930s. Built in 1843, it was closed shortly after the Second World War.

The site remained vacant for many years but now forms part of Craigmill Park.

The row of colliery houses at Cambois known as Boca Chica. The Methodist Chapel can be seen at the end of the street on the extreme left. The houses were demolished in the 1970s but the chapel remained, being used as a Boys' Club. The remaining buildings including the Boys' Club and the Ridley Arms public house (known locally as the 'Willick') were demolished in 1996.

The land, from West Bridge Street to the former High Ferry Landing including Hughes Bolkow's the shipbreakers, has been fenced off after being excavated to a great depth to dispose of asbestos and highly toxic chemicals so that it could be re-used. Today scrap metal is exported from the new jetty where ships were once broken up.

COMMERCE

T&S Mole Cycle Dealers on Regent Street, Cowpen Quay in 1902. The three men in the centre of the photograph are John Mole with his sons Alfred Septimus and Tom on either side of him. They were the sole makers of the 'Northumbrians' the only bicycles built in Blyth, which were priced between £8 10s 0d and £12 12s 0d. Other makes in stock included Enfields, Rovers, Stars, Triumph, Wearwell and Fleet cycles.

Soulsby's

Robert Soulsby's the butchers were one of the oldest established butchers in the town. Robert senior broke away from his brother George, also a butcher, to set up by himself and eventually his sons, Robert jnr, Arthur Hughie, Edwin, William and George, as well as their sister took over the business. They owned four different shops in Blyth, with the one in Waterloo Road, now an oriental restaurant becoming the main one as the others were closed. They also had six red vans that traded all over South East Northumberland. They were commonly known as the 'Red Soulsbys'. George Soulsby, who traded in the Market Place had blue vans and was known as 'Blue Soulsby'.

Note the bulls' heads under the name. Sides of beef hung outside are no longer seen. Rules of hygiene having drastically changed. The shop was subsequently Ashby's, then Crowe & Atkinson (now trading in Bowes Street).

The two businesses trading side by side in Market Street between the Market Inn and Woolworth's in the 1920s. The '3d' above the Woolworth's store can be seen on the right. Woolworth's were famous for being the '3d and 6d' store.

Robert Soulsby's shop in Market Street.

Robert Soulsby's van in Waterloo Road. George Soulsby is the driver.

Robson's

Robson Brothers began trading in Blyth in 1904, in premises which are now the Trustees Savings Bank in Waterloo Road. The business was begun by George Charlton Robson and his brothers, Thomas and William – who

The staff of Robson's Boot and Shoe Store.

was a sleeping partner. George was unfortunately killed in 1918 in an accident at Cambois when the horse-drawn trap he was driving crashed into a lamppost after the horse bolted. Another brother, Fred, then joined the business, working in the boot and shoe factory. Around this time more than 20 men and boys were working in the factory, in the shop six women were employed to serve the customers. The company moved to its present location when Cummings, another repair company, moved out. The repair factory was upstairs where it remained until it was closed in 1974. The company, now in Waterloo Road, is still in the ownership of the family.

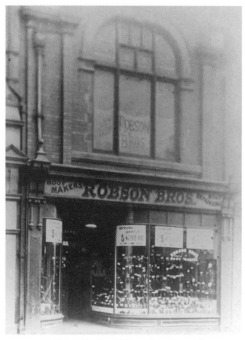

Robson's in Waterloo Road.

The premises today.

Two views of Regent Street taken from Station Street. These photographs, taken before to the First World War, show three of the many businesses that once occupied this very busy street, Taylor's provision merchants, Lees newsagents and Archibald-Ramsden's musical instrument shop.

Below: In 1999, First Freeze occupy the site. They took over from Job Lot who purchased the site from the Coronation Social Club.

Breyen, Richardson & Co on the corner of Ridley Street and the then Market Street, pre 1914.

The building is now used for selling cars and accessories.

Blyth Timber Merchants G & N Wright's original yard in Bridge Street. G & N Wright eventually moved to a site off Wensleydale Terrace adjoining the harbour where timber could be unloaded directly from ships into their facilities. The business prospered for many years but was eventually sold to Malden Timber, who subsequently closed the yard and moved to a new site on the Blyth Industrial Estate off Cowpen Road.

The site is now occupied by the Bus Station.

The Tower Lodging House and Richard Conrad Bush's Garage in the 1960s. The Tower Garage was taken over in April 1962, after the death of the original owner Mr Joseph Jennings Smith. The new owners were George William Allison and Richard C. Bush. The name of the Garage was changed from 'Tower Garage' to 'Tower Garage and Coach Works'. The new owners were qualified panel beaters and painters by trade. The original Tower Garage was established before the Second World War by a company called C & H Gibson who dealt in taxis and private hire. Messrs Allison and Bush became partners with a view of establishing the coach works. After two years Mr Allison left the company. Since then the garage and coach works business has developed significantly by the acquisition of land from Blyth Valley Borough Council on which modern workshops and facilities have been built.

The company, whilst still being a private family business run by Mr Bush and his wife Irene, still remains at the same location making it the oldest garage in Blyth Town Centre. Today, the business specialises as recovery agents for Northumbria Police, Green Flag, GESA, Mondial and an independent motor body repairer with insurance company appointments.

The west end of Waterloo Road in the 1960s. On the left is Robert Soulsby's butchers shop with its bakery above. Next to that is Maxwell's high class grocers and a little further up the street is Leask's sweet shop. In the right foreground is the Prince of Wales public house with its once familiar red GPO telephone box. The shop blind visible beyond is that of the Co-Op chemist. The photographer is standing under the blind of Bell's the florist, now Forget-Me-Not.

Today, the Co-Op Funeral Home adjoins the Great Emperor Chinese Restaurant and the Arthritis Research Charity Shop is next. The Prince of Wales remains but the chemist is now a Motor Accessory shop – Motor World.

South side staithes, the entrance to Colpitts' Yard, *circa* 1960.

J.W. Colpitts & Co Ltd, established in 1890. These premises were destroyed by fire in 1988 and the site is now occupied by light industrial workshops. This is known locally as 'Colpitts' Corner'. The company were marine and general engineers but marine engineering made up almost 100 per cent of the work when the port was busy and thriving.

The view today where the staithes once stood. One of the new wind turbines (North Pier) is visible.

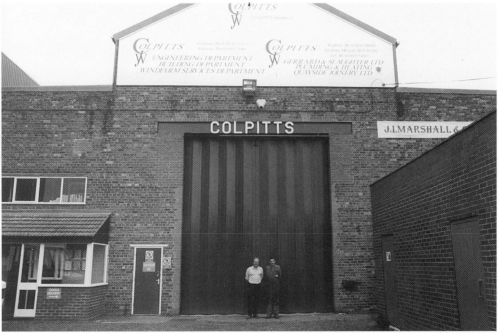

The present 'Colpitts' facility with production manager, Tommy Orr and the company's oldest serving employee, Harry A'Court on the right. Today, marine work accounts for only two per cent of the company's work. Ownership of the company changed in 1978 when George Colpitts, Bessie Holgeth (née Colpitts) and Charles Holgeth retired. After the 1988 fire, the company moved into the Plumbers, Tinsmiths and Foundry premises of the former Blyth Shipbuilding and Dry Dock Company, bringing back engineering work to the site of the shipyard. Due to expansion it now has interests in custom joinery and the Morpeth plumbing company, Gerard and Slaughter. It has maintenance contracts with the Blyth Harbour Windfarm, Morrisons Supermarkets and Vald Birn (UK) Ltd.

This shop was on the corner of Turner Street (now Regent Street) and Simpson Street, *circa* 1919. The shop was owned by Smithson's who sold decorating materials and also operated a painting and decorating business. The boy in the photograph is Will Stannard.

The shop is now a formal hire business, having previously been a travel agent, a florist's and a radio and television shop.

This short block of shops ran between Disraeli Street and Salisbury Street. The photograph shows the buildings in the process of demolition in the mid 1970s. Some who ran their businesses from these premises included: Alfie Boast's men's outfitter, John Mather's Post Office and newsagents, Arthur Fail the butcher, Les Mackin painter and decorator, and Eric Routledge plumber. Ralph Allen took over the Post Office in 1963. Ralph had been a professional footballer and was leading goalscorer for Charlton Athletic in the 1935-36 and 1936-37 seasons – scoring 24 goals in each. A prolific centre forward, he was at Brentford before moving to Charlton. He went on to play for Fulham, Torquay and Reading, before becoming a publican and then a post master. Ralph had followed his brother Jack into football. Jack played for Newcastle United and scored both goals in the 1932 FA Cup Final when the Magpies beat Arsenal 2-1 at Wembley.

The area today has changed completely with Tower Garage and Coach Works occupying most of the site. The forecourt being used by John F. Hay for second hand car sales. Jill's Dog Grooming Parlour also forms part of the complex.

Thomas York's butcher shop on the corner of Regent Street and Wright Street, *circa* 1910. The man wearing the striped apron was John Burdon Dorwood, who eventually took over the business. The two little girls were his daughters Nellie and Maggie. The lad on the corner was his son Jack. The shop was demolished and an office belonging to the DHSS was built there. More recently it was owned by Ladbrokes the bookmakers but is now empty.

A view looking west up Bridge Street, towards Waterloo Road in 1987. On the left is Albion House occupied by Thoms Discount Store. This store was once a major department store owned by the GUS group who purchased it from the previous owner Mr Young. The business traded under the name Hedley and Young; Mr Hedley being the founding owner. The building was constructed by local builders J&W Simpson. On the right is the Central Methodist Church, which was demolished to make way for the Keel Row Shopping Centre which also took in the adjoining properties which were occupied by Walter Willsons the grocers, Dorothy's Ladies and Children's Wear, Marshall's the bakers and Marcus Price Men's Wear. In Trotter Street, behind the church, stood the Alexandra Billiard Hall and Centre 64, the Methodist Youth Club, both now demolished.

The scene today. Albion House remains but trades under the name Pound Stretchers, and a video hire shop. The new shopping centre dominates the site of the church.

Green's Stores on the corner of Bridge Street and Quay Road in the late 1930s. Only four members of the staff in the photograph can be identified, they are: Olga Bakes (née Thompson), fifth from the left; Margaret Dawson, seventh from the left; the two men in the doorway are, left to right, Sidney Hudson and Mr Green; and on the extreme right is Mr Ball.

The site is now occupied by the Arriva Bus Garage formerly the United Bus Company's Garage.

CHURCHES

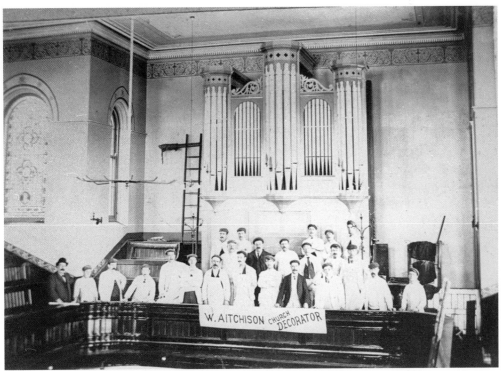

Decorating the Wesleyan Chapel (Central Methodist Church), 1903.
W. Aitchison covered every area of painting and decorating including ships.
His business premises were in Station Street, Cowpen Quay and he lived at 16
Marine Terrace. One of the painters in the middle of the second row was John
Herron who later established his own decorating business in Blyth – T. Herron
& Son.

St Cuthbert's Church – Church of England

In 1751 the 'Blyth Church' was commissioned by the Ridley family as a Chapel of Ease to the parish church of Earsdon. This building was never consecrated. Sir Matthew White Ridley gave the church in 'trust' to the Diocesan Society in 1883 and it was separated from the Parish of Earsdon.

The foundation stone of the present church was laid in August 1884. The building was consecrated in 1885 and finally completed in 1892.

The Chapel of Ease, built in 1751. It was demolished in 1925 to make way for the Parish Hall. William Carr the 'strong man' of Blyth is buried in the churchyard.

St Cuthbert's C. of E. Church, 1998. Originally a weather cock and four pinnacles decorated the tower, but following a severe gale in 1937 these were removed, one of the pinnacles having damaged the nave roof.

The interior of St Cuthbert's Church, 1926.

The interior of St Cuthbert's, 1998.

St Cuthbert's Church Choir, *circa* 1948. Back row, left to right: ? Wade, ? Wade, R. Madgwick, R. Aldcroft, unknown, H. Shaw, W. Mills, unknown, unknown. Middle row: A. Gibson, unknown, S. Fulbeck, E. Dixon, G. Dixon, J. Crichenson, C. Davison, H. Madgwick, P. Thompson. Front row: unknown, G. Amory. K. Gibson, unknown, M. Kelsey, Revd Mann, L. Crichenson, H. Usher, R. Wheatley, G. Amory.

St Cuthbert's Church Choir, 1998. Included in this photograph are: S. Dawson, J. Straker, J. Allen, S. Laws, S. Cooper, M. Henderson, J. Turnbull, H. Davison, V. Jackson, P. Graysmark, D. Cooper, S. Anderson, S. Smith, J. Kulke, C. Davison, M. Hunter (Choir Mistress), D. Anderson, R. Dodds (Organist), S. Anderson, C. Smith. The Revd K. Young officiating during the interregnum. The Revd R. Taylor is now priest in charge of St Cuthbert's.

St Mary's Church – Church of England

The Parish Church of St Mary was originally built as a Chapel of Ease to the Parish Church of St Mary, Horton, which had been taken out of the enormous Parish of Woodhorn in January 1769.

This chapel was the result of the educational concerns of William Greenwell who had become Perpetual Curate of Horton in 1856. Because of his interest and concern the Trustees of Thoroton and Croft, owners of most of Cowpen and who were enlarging the new suburb of Waterloo begun in 1822, responded to his enthusiasm and gifted a parcel of land in the centre of Waterloo for the building of a schoolroom, a parsonage and a chapel.

The National School (Cowpen Church of England School) was opened in April 1860. Descendants of pupils of this school still worship at St Mary's. It ceased to be a school in 1914/15. The building became the Church Hall and was used until the 1980s when it was demolished and sold to developers. The site is now occupied by Argos and a branch of the Northumberland College of Further Education. A new hall was built adjoining the Baptistery at the west end of the church.

The headmaster's house, subsequently living accommodation for a verger and then a caretaker, is a listed building and provides offices for a firm of financial consultants.

The Chapel of St Mary was consecrated in June 1864 and the first extensions were begun in 1897 and were dedicated Easter 1903.

In 1898 the Thoroton and Croft Trustees offered a site in Cowpen Quay for a proposed new mission (St John's). It was bought for two shillings (10p) per yard. The Mission Room was opened by the Bishop in July 1901 and served the parishioners of Cowpen Quay. By 1957 the worshippers had permanently joined the congregation at St Mary's. The building no longer exists.

St Mary's East End, 1962.

St Mary's East End, Lent 1998.

St Mary's, *circa* 1909. Behind the tree on the left can be seen the original
school building.

St Mary's Choir and Servers, 1931. Included are: G. Newall, T. Noble, T. Ridley,
N. Gibson, H. Hurrell, J. Straughan, M. Bates, S. Hately, J. Mahler, R. Muter
(Organist), R. Shanks, G. Thompson, J. Ross, N. Bilton, A. Carnaby,
H. Wyergang, T. Straughan, J. Patterson, G. Smith, O. Hall, L. Bates,
J. Kennedy, J. Brison, B. Newall, D. Wilkinson, W. Hurrell, G. Archer,
J. Tuttiett, W. Adams, Dr L.L. Steele (Church Warden), Revd W. Sambridge
(Curate), Revd C.F. Medd (Vicar), O. Robinson, J.W. Hogarth (Church
Warden), D. Watts, L. Hall, R. Steele, E. Straughan, A. Trimble, C. Smith,
H. Swann.

St Mary's, 1998. The new church hall can be seen to the left, it was officially opened 27th January 1991.

St Mary's Choir and Servers, 1952. Clergy – Vicar, The Revd F.G.C. Mathew (centre), The Revd C. Horton (left), The Revd D. Simpson (right). Included are: T. Carter, T. Hoskins, A. Mayes, E. Whiteman, F. Widdas, G. Laird, C. Smith, R. Steele, A. Cole, R. Young, N. Weedy, N. Rae, A. Wellington, R. Robertson, W. Lambert, G. Shepherd, A. Herron, I. Wellington, E. Hume, J. Mason, J. Pringle, K. Robson, F. Oakley, N. Walker, R. Walker, B. Nicholson, J. Bower, A. Carr, J. Bell, K. Lee, G. Davison, R. Blackett, A. Thomas, J. Campbell, J. Jones, N. Carragan, C. Beattie, K. Mason.

St Mary's Servers, 1998. Back row: G. Holmes, J. Brennand, J. McLeod. Middle row: I. Davidson, K. Fitch, J. Crowe, R. Wake, M. Smith, R. Davidson. Front row: E. Whiteman, A. Brennand (Church Warden), Revd B. Benison (Vicar & Rural Dean), W. Wheatley (Church Warden), A. Mayes.

The growth and development of the town from a handful of cottages situated at what was known as South Blyth is reflected in the building of churches and the establishment of meeting places for various religious groups.

Before 1751 there is no evidence of the existence of places of Religious Instruction in South Blyth which was one of the eight townships in the Chapelry of Earsdon. The inhabitants were expected to travel either to Earsdon or Horton for marriages, baptisms and funerals.

Until the See of Newcastle was formed in 1882 Blyth, with the rest of Northumberland lay in the Diocese of Durham.

A Catholic Chapel was attached to the Manor House of Newsham (the barn of North Farm on South Newsham Road is built on the site of the house which was demolished in 1880), and it is possible that the people were allowed to worship there, however there is no known record of this.

The chapel was there in 1586 when the house was occupied by John Ogle but there is no mention of a priest. Possibly the chaplain to Sir John Delaval attended to the spiritual needs of the few inhabitants of Newsham and Blyth Nook.

Church of St Wilfrid's and Our Lady – Roman Catholic

In the sixteenth and seventeenth century there were Roman Catholic connections with the Ogles of Newsham Manor and the Delaval family. The penal laws against 'Catholics' came into being which continued until the reign of George IV. Priests were banished, anyone helping or protecting them were breaking the law. Many were executed. Although none were executed there were known 'papists' in Newsham and Blyth.

When Queen Victoria came to the throne in 1837 the Roman Catholic Mass was said in a room in the Sidney Arms at Cowpen and later in a house called Cowpen Grove. J.F. Sidney erected the present Cowpen R.C. Chapel in 1840. The Church of St Wilfrid was opened in 1864 and served by priests of the English Benedictine Order. St Wilfrid's is considered to have the finest stained glass of any church in Blyth.

St Wilfrid's and our Lady R.C. Church, Waterloo Road.

The original Presbytery.

The shrine erected in the 1970s, beautifully kept by the nuns who came to live in the Presbytery after the Convent of St Mary at Fenham was closed.

After years of service, and being held in respect and affection by the whole community, the nuns are now living in various parts of the country and are greatly missed.

A house on the opposite side of Waterloo Road, originally built by Dr Charles Fairlie, was acquired to house the priest Fr. James Lennon.

Below: Nuns at St Wilfrid's, 1998. Back row: Sister Mary Standish, Sister Joan Doherty, Sister Kathleen Kenny, Sister Flora McDonald. Front row: Sister Mary Mackin, Sister Margaret Tournour.

The interior of St Wilfrid's
before alterations in the 1960s.

The interior of St Wilfrid's,
1998.

St Cuthbert's R.C. Church, Cowpen.

The interior of St Cuthbert's Church. The exact date is unknown but it is probably the 1930s.

Non Conformist Congregations

Methodists

On Good Friday and Easter Monday 1743 John Wesley preached to local miners at Plessey and a youth named William Hunter was so impressed and influenced by him he became a local preacher. He began a mission about 1791 and preached in the open air to miners. Until 1804, when a permanent building was hired, the services were held in various rooms in the area.

A chapel was built on Ballast Hill in 1815 which served until 1867 when the larger chapel, which became known as the Central Methodist Church, was built at Blyth Bridge.

The old Wesleyan Chapel on Ballast Hill became known as the Norwegian Chapel. This dated from the time when Norwegian seamen in port attended the chapel.

Methodists of the New Connexion (Zion Methodists) sprang from a sermon given by the Revd Alexander Kilhaw who had been ejected from the Wesleyan parent body in 1796 over principles of church government. The first preaching place was a cottage in Cowpen Square belonging to Richard Hodgson. Between 1804 and 1815 they shared a room near the Dun Cow Inn with the Wesleyans.

The Zion Methodist Church in Waterloo Road.

In 1818 a chapel was built in Waterloo Road called the Zion Chapel where the old Theatre Royal later stood. This building was replaced in 1866 by another chapel on Waterloo Road, subsequently demolished for the present market development.

During the Second World War the schoolroom was commandeered by the military and used by the Home Guard.

There were several Methodist churches in the town but as areas of housing were demolished congregations shrank and eventually the Central Methodist Church became the centre of all Methodist worship. The church opened for services in 1869.

This landmark building was replaced by the present church in Beaconsfield Street which was officially opened in 1990.

The site of the Bridge Street Church is now part of the Keel Row Shopping Precinct.

BLYTH CENTRAL METHODIST CHURCH
BEACONSFIELD STREET.

A SERVICE TO CELEBRATE THE

Official Opening

to be held in the New Church
SATURDAY, 24th. NOVEMBER 1990

Speaker :   Mr. ALAN BEITH. M.P.
Chairman :   The Rev. ALEC CALLABY

TEA 4. 00p m. for 4. 30p.m.   SERVICE commences 7. 00p.m.

An invitation to the official opening of Blyth Central Methodist Church, Beaconsfield Street, Saturday, 24th November 1990.

At the opening, left to right: Mr A. Beith MP, Revd D. MacDonald, Revd A. Callaby (Blyth Minister), The Revd Canon M. Nelson (St Mary's Blyth), Revd B. Cash (Seaton Delaval).

Central Methodist Church, Bridge Street.

Wimpy now occupies the site of the Central Methodist Church.

Central Methodist Church, Beaconsfield Street. The first service was held on 28th November 1990.

The interior of New Church in Beaconsfield Street.

The interior of the Central Methodist Church, Bridge Street.

Central Methodist Choir, 1962. Back row: A. Robson, N. Dodds, L. Loud, J. Scougal, I. Preacher, A. Phillipson, G. Smith (choir mistress), C. Dobson, L. Henderson, J. Johnson, Revd J. Spencer, J. Ferguson, J. Hallett, M. Bagley, W. Henderson, B. English. Front row: P. Turnbull, I. Wilkinson, M. Jewels, C. Robson, J. Bradley, P. Raffell, N. Laws, O. Gardiner, K. Moorhead, M. Crosby.

Central Methodist Church Choir, March 1999. Back row: G. Dady, D. Henderson, W. Ferguson, F. Rockett. Middle row: A. Madgewick, L. Robson, T. Armstrong, J. Hebron, N. Pottie, C. Rockett, A. Martin, D. Martin. Front row: H. Golightly, O. Gardner, K. Saddler, E. Dady, Revd G. Scarlett, P. Turnbull, J. Anderson.

Another prominent Methodist Chapel was that of the Primitive Methodists in Beaconsfield Street opened in 1913; now replaced by the Phoenix Theatre (below).

New Delaval Christian Lay Church – the 'Lay Chapel'. The church was established in 1883 and rebuilt in 1902, it is situated between the present New Delaval First School and the Golf Course. As the title indicates it is run entirely by a lay congregation.

The United Reformed Church formerly the Presbyterian.

It seems highly probable that this movement and congregation started in the 1770s under the Revd Thomas Craig, schoolmaster and Protestant Reformatory Minister and was well established by the 1780s meeting in a room above the rope warehouse in Queen's Lane.

The first permanent building was in Church Street known as the 'Ebeneezer' Chapel, completed in 1814, and which included a schoolroom. It was used as a place of worship for 60 years; after which it became the home of the Scientific Institute until it was demolished to make way for the Police Station.

The United Presbyterians built a new church in Bridge Street in 1863. A decline in church numbers caused the closure of this building in 1944 after which it became a factory for the making of mineral water. Bridge House now stands on this site.

In 1876 the Presbyterian Church of England was opened in Waterloo Road. The spire of this building providing a very useful landmark, and when the Bridge Street Church closed it provided the centre for all Presbyterian worship. In 1972 the Presbyterians and Congregationalists amalgamated forming the United Reformed Church.

The Presbyterian Church in Waterloo Road.

The church in 1998, now the United Reform Church. Restoration work is being carried out on the spire.

The interior of the Church of St Bede, Newsham. The church was consecrated in 1957. The present St Bede's Church is the fourth building of that name, the present Church Hall and Community Centre being the third and until the present church was built was used for both  recreation and worship. During the erection of this building, an army hut (where the care park now is) was used as a church – one of the author's was baptised at three weeks old in that hut. The first church was situated at the 'top' of the colliery (New Delaval) and served the Anglican Community between 1888 and 1920. All weddings, however, were solemnised at St Mary's, Horton. St Bede's was not licensed for marriages until 1947. The materials for the first church were donated by the Seaton Delaval Coal Company.

The present St Bede's Church.

SCHOOLDAYS

Blyth Secondary School for Girls, House Captains, 1927. Left to right: Edith Thompson, Issie Parker, Mary Shy, Eva Straughan. The building became Blyth Grammar School and is now Delaval Middle School.

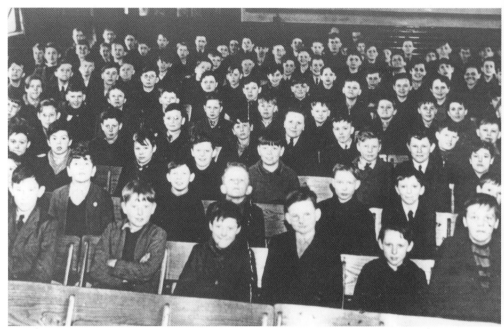

Pupils of Princess Louise Road Boys Secondary School, 1945.

Princess Louise Road Senior School Football Team, 1937-38. Back row, left to right: Ted Patterson, Frank Oakley, Jacky Williamson, Stan Mordue, Bill Allen, Ron Towers, Ellison Sutherland, Albony Battonsby, Tommy Harrison. Second row: Johnny Adams, Ronnie English, Jimmy Kennedy, Dennis Stokoe, Gerald Kelly (teacher), Bill Golding, Bill Dawson (teacher), Stanley Parker, Alec Cunningham, Alan Gibson, Norman Johnson. Third row: Stan Cavers, Kenny Allen, Ronnie Taggart, Arnold Pawson, Tommy Soulsby, Ronnie Dryden. Front row: Ken Stobbs, George Amory, Bobby Bruce, Ronald Rutter.

Princess Louise Road Infants School, Class 6, 1952.

Princess Louise Road Infants School Staff, 1955. Back row: Miss Windle, Mrs Dixon. Front row: Mrs A. Drury, Mrs I Butters, Miss I. Whitelaw (headmistress), Miss J. Athey, Mrs J. Oxley.

'Bon Accord' Private School, *circa* 1900. It was situated in the centre section of Bondicar Terrace, which at this time was known as Grey Street. The young lady second from the right is Miss Margaret Potts who married the decorator T. Herron.

Blyth Grammar School 1st XI, 1952-53. They played 21 games, won 17, drew 1, lost 3, goals 100-21. Back row, left to right: Mr Proctor, P. Hawkes, F. Taylor, B. Davies, A. Patience, K. Davey, R. Nesbit, R. Curry. Front row: W. Gilbert, D. Henderson, P. Butters, J. Riddell, R. Knight.

Blyth Secondary School Girls Choir, 1928. Included in the back row: M. Smith, H. Mullarkley, M. Denton, K. Bloxam, H. Easton, E. Farrell, E. Smith, M. Shy, S, Wright. Middle row: I. Parker, N. Lynn, H. Mitcheson, E. Straughan, Mr Wyatt, K. Swann, unknown, P. Ferrell, unknown, L. Dixon. Front row: E. Henderson, ? Shields, M. Bligh, M. Crowe, L. Henderson.

A group of Blyth children near Bebside Pit Heap.

New Delaval Infants School, 1951. Built in 1874 by the Seaton Delaval Coal Company, it was demolished when the surrounding land became Blyth Golf Course and the present Club Building was erected.

The scene today.

New Delaval Infants School, Class 3, 1951, with Head Teacher, Miss Elizabeth Pattison.

Class 2 with Deputy Head, Miss Constance Atkinson in 1951.

Class 1 in 1951 with Miss Muriel Dodds who became Mrs Woodcock.

Blyth Schools FA, 1935-36. This was the team that reached the semi-finals of the English Schools Boys' Cup against West Ham. They played a 1-1 draw at Croft Park, but were well beaten 4-0 in the return game in London. Back row: J. Pearson (teacher), J. Hooper (New Delaval), B. Coulson (teacher), H. Mills (St Wilfrid's), W. Dawson (teacher), W. Emery (Grammar). Middle row: Alderman T.C. Black, W. Milburn (Grammar), T. Downing (New Delaval), D. Wilson - captain (Grammar), R. Walton (New Delaval), F. Mitchell (teacher), R. Robertson (teacher). Front row: G. Hudson (Foster Senior), F. Hertwick (P.L.R.), Fred Chapple (P.L.R.), Councillor J.W. Heatley JP, S. Riddle (Foster Senior), Alderman Reilly, N. Branigan (P.L.R.), J. Thompson (Grammar), ? Laker (New Delaval). Late in the game at Croft Park, Blyth were awarded a penalty. Wilson took the kick, the West Ham goalkeeper, Gregory, dived the wrong way but the ball struck his foot and flew to safety. Gregory went on to play for West Ham United and became one of their longest serving players. Jimmy Thompson played for the England School Boys but was killed on active service with the Royal Air Force whilst flying over Germany during the Second World War. Fred Chapple had trials with England School Boys.

Blyth Town Juniors, 1998-99. Back row: Neil Watson, Andrew Wylam, Garry White, Gary Easton, David Bell, Andrew Adamson, Andrew Reed, Alan Beresford. Front row: James Patterson, Kevin Welsh, Daniel Beresford, Mark Wilson (captain), John Charlton, Dean Moat.

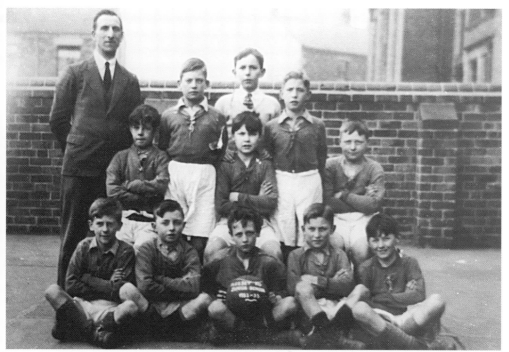

Plessey Road Junior School Football Team, 1932-33. Back row: Mr Pearson, Ray Crawford, Bill Soulsby, John Bushel. Middle row: Tommy Dean, Alfie Armstrong, Tom Harrison. Front row: Fred Hertwick, ? Patterson, Fred Chapple, Norman Branigan and Jimmy Thompson.

Plessey Road County First School Football Team, 1998-99. Back row: Mr C. Bell, Christopher Jobson, Tony Lennie, Dan Rowley, Ian Greenacre, Stephen Saddler, Charles Brown, Jake Grebhard, Mark Yeoman and Mr K. Douglas. Middle row: Jill Soulsby, Callum Adam, Liam Rowley, Stephen Long. Front row: Garry McMorland, Neil McDonald.

Plessey Road School, class of 1919.

Plessey Road School, class of 1998. Front row: Neil McDonald, Gary McMorland, Gemma Moses, Callum Adam, Anthony Linney. Second Row: Jessica Cunningham, Rachel Brown, Robyn Irvine, Laura Rutherford, Charles Brown, Andrew Walker, Alec Foster, Allyson Leslie, Katherine Howe, Melissa Douglas, Rebecca Laing, Samantha Tulip. Third Row: Mrs C. McMillan, John Bowery, Oliver Wilkinson, Ian Greenacre, Danny Black, Rachel Bestford, Jill Soulsby, Stephen Long, Liam Rowley, David Watson, Martin Young. Back row: Rachel Robinson, Scott Oliver, Andrew Pitkeathly, Laura Parkin, Stephen Saddler, Tony Lennie, Dan Rowley, Thomas Crate, Karl Rose, Mr C. Bell.

PORT AND HARBOUR

Tommy Pearson, Ronnie Fairless and Bill Taylor – joiners working at Blyth Dry Docks & Shipbuilding Co., 1960.

Port and Harbour

As early as the thirteenth century, salt was traded on the River Blyth. Evaporation of brine needed coal which was available in shallow seams near Cowpen.

The development and business of the coal trade on the river is well known and documented. The foundations of the trade were laid early in the eighteenth century when the industrial history of the port really began. One of the first English railways was laid down between Bebside Colliery and the river. There were beams of wood, along which coal wagons were drawn by horses. Blyth become the fourth coal shipping port in England in the eighteenth century.

The harbour had for long been referred to by mariners as 'Abraham's Bosom' because it was a safe haven in stormy weather. The port's busy past was based on iron, coal, shipbuilding, ship repairing and ship breaking. Aluminium has given it a new lease of life after spells of grain and timber exporting and the import of paper.

The river mouth is now dominated by the chimneys of Cambois Power Station and more recently by the windmills of the Wind Farm.

Commissioners Offices, Blyth

The harbour and port has been consistently improved and maintained throughout the years by the Harbour Commissioners. A site was chosen on the corner of Blagdon Street for their offices. The building was opened by the 2nd Viscount Ridley in 1913. The building on the left is part of Keenlyeside's the Ships' Chandlers, now demolished.

Blyth Harbour Entrance

The Harbour entrance, *circa* 1890. On the left can be seen the construction work for the pier known as the Blyth Wooden pier. The pier in the centre is the Inner West or Harbour Master's Pier. This was shortened after Blyth pier was constructed but its former end can still be distinguished by a marker with a red light in the harbour entrance.

The view of the entrance today is completely different with the wind turbines dominating the skyline to the right of the photograph. The silos of the Alcan jetty can also be seen in the background.

South Harbour

Dockers unloading lengths of pine trees imported from Scandinavia for use in the coal mines. The 'pit props' were used to shore-up the roof at the coal face. The land now used as the Harbour Commission Caravan and Boat Park was where the timber was stacked until needed. This area was known as the 'Prop Yard'. After mechanisation of the mining industry, mechanical props almost ended the use of timber props.

The Ro-Ro terminal today in the South Harbour with one of the regular visiting ships. The two small boats on the left of the photograph are the Harbour Master's and Pilots' Launch while the other boat is the old pilot cutter. The Ro-Ro boats bring in mainly paper products to the South Harbour, retaining the link with Scandinavia. Containers are lifted from boats by the large crane in the background. There is also a small trade in fertiliser imports. Exports include Nissan motor cars from the Sunderland factory and Aluminium ingots from the Lynemouth smelter.

Since 1890 an area of the South Harbour has been the headquarters of the Royal Northumberland Yacht Club. However, more recently the club house boat *Tyne* has been moved to a more secure position by the middle jetty and a gate erected for security reasons. A series of pontoons have been built making mooring and access easier (below).

The four masted steel Barque *Cap Horn* loading coal at the Cowpen Coal Company staithes at North Blyth. The ship was French owned but was built in Port Glasgow in 1888.

In 1999 the staithes have gone, replaced by the Alcan unloading facility which was built in 1970. A suction system is used to unload the various cargoes that are stored in giant silos before being transported by rail to the company's smelter at Lynemouth.

The steamship *Fairy* loading at South Side Staithes, 1910. The *Fairy* was built in 1902 and owned by the East Coast Steamship Co. of Kings Lynn. The staithes were demolished in the 1960s.

The scene today. On the left is the oiling jetty, behind it is the disused Customs House. In the centre are the former premises of Bell, Dunn and Keenlyside – Ships' Chandlers – then the Maritime Buildings which housed the offices of the many shipbrokers involved in the business of the port.

Blyth Harbour West Basin, *circa* 1950s. The Golden Fleece public house can be seen on the left. Bates Colliery Coal Loading Facility with one ship alongside loading, and another lying astern awaiting her turn are also on the left. The West Staithes with a ship loading coal can be seen in the centre. The ship to the right is being demolished at Hughes Bolkow's Shipbreaking Yard. The flat bottomed vehicle and passenger ferry which hauled itself to and fro across the river between Blyth and Cambois using two heavy cables strung from one side to the other can be seen on the right. When a ship sailed up the river to the West Basin she was required to blow a long and two shorts on her whistle to give the ferry man time to drop the cables on to the river bed to let the ship pass over them.

The Golden Fleece Inn in Ann's Row, High Ferry Landing, *circa* 1950.

Blyth Harbour West Basin today. This photograph was taken from the bridge of
the Finnish M.V. *Camilla*, unloading paper at the Roll-On-Roll-Off jetty at
Wimbourne Quay. The Ro-Ro jetty rises and falls with the tide allowing the
loading and unloading to continue without pause. One of the tractors used in
the operation can be seen reversing a flat trailer into the hold of the ship to be
loaded with huge reels of paper used in the newspaper industry.

The Golden Fleece public house can again be seen on the left having
undergone several face lifts over the years, the most recent in 1996 when a
brick and glass conservatory was built allowing customers to eat and drink
whilst enjoying one of the best views of the river.

Bates Loading Facility still remains and is now used for the export of grain,
gravel and open cast coal. Blyth Harbour Commission has a lease on the
equipment dominating the sky line. The chimneys of Blyth 'A' and 'B' Power
Stations can also be seen. 'A' is on the right, 'B' on the left.

The west staithes were cut down in 1995 leaving just a jetty. The remaining
quay was cut back 100 metres to create a bigger basin for ships to swing. The
ship lying at the former Hughes Bolkows Shipbreakers Yard is loading scrap
metal for export to Spain.

Dredgers

In 1913 a self-propelled hopper dredger was acquired to aid the work of deepening and maintaining the channel.

There have been several dredgers used in the port with names like *Blyth*, *Cambois* and *Cowpen*. The last dredger, the *Crofton*, is shown above. She is of the suction type. The *Crofton* last worked in the port in 1998 before moving to Fleetwood. The port no longer has its own dredger. The task of dredging the river is now contracted out to a Dutch company. The Harbour Commissioners only use a plough. The harbour tug, *Blyth Endeavour*, drags the plough along the river bed close to the quays, dragging the spoil into the centre of the river to be picked up by a suction dredger.

Pilot Cutters

Blyth Pilots were once self-employed ex-sea captains who owned their own boats. They boarded incoming and outgoing ships, steering them safely in and out of the harbour. In 1954, when the Port was exporting millions of tons of coal, there were 31 pilots. Now forty-five years later there are only three, plus the Harbour Master who also does a watch. The Pilotage was taken over by the Harbour Commissioners during the late 1980s. They now employ the Harbour Master and Pilots. The present boat (below) now has a dual role as Pilot Cutter and Harbour Master's Launch.

Shipbuilding

The shipbuilding industry started in Blyth in the eighteenth century when in 1750 Edmund Hannay started to build ships. About the same time, Edward Watts (son-in-law of Hannay) established a shipyard on the Blyth side of the flanker. From 1881, iron and steel ships were built regularly at Blyth until the official closure of the yard in 1966.

The *King Theseus* ready for launch in 1957. The owners were the Theseus Shipping Co. Ltd and she was registered in Piraeus, Greece.

Ships on the slips. The *Plumleaf* built in 1960 and the *Queensgarth* built in 1959.

The launch of the tanker, *Plumleaf*, built by the Blyth Dry Dock and Shipbuilding Co. in 1960.

The launch of the *Hamilton Trader*, at Blyth, 23rd July 1959.

Hamilton Trader in dry dock on the River Tyne during final painting.

HMS *Blyth*, built in 1941/42, was a Bangor Class, Fleet Mine Sweeper. In charge was Commander Temple, the CO of the 16th Mine Sweeping Flotilla. The ship's first task was to sweep the Channel to enable the battleship, *King George V* to leave the Tyne. The *Blyth* survived the war and it was planned to change the name to *Radbourne* in preparation for it being converted for use as a weather ship. However, the conversion was never completed and it was scrapped in 1949. This photograph was taken while carrying out compass adjusting in the bay at Blyth. The figure high up in the crow's nest is Jim Beamish who is a resident of Blyth today.

A ship in the Dry Dock for repairs during the Second World War. The coal staithes can be seen in the background.

The Dry Docks

The area occupied by the former Blyth shipyard in 1907 showing all six dry docks in use and ships tied up alongside.

This photograph, taken in 1999, shows the same area as shown above but the Dry Docks and slipways have been filled in and replaced by sheds which are used to store paper brought into the port from Scandinavia. The number 1 and 2 Dry Docks are still in use. The sluice gates remain closed and the docks are full of water. They are used in the development of undersea submersibles for use in pipeline inspection work and repair in the offshore gas and oil industry, and for the training of associated staff.

Blyth Dry Docks 1 and 2, 1907.

The scene today.

Shipbreaking

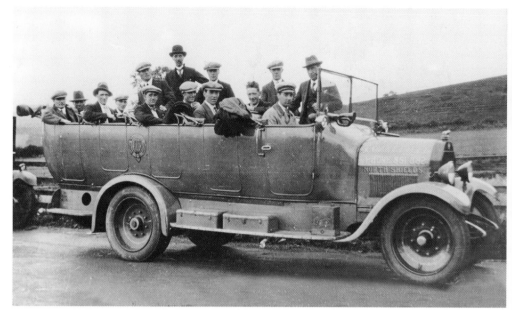

Hughes Bolkow's employees' outing, early in the century. Hughes Bolkow began breaking up ships at Battleship Wharf in 1912. Previously they had a dismantling quay on the Tyne. Shipbreaking is an excellent example of re-cycling. For example some of the steel recovered from the *Mauritania*, broken up in 1935, became part of the plates of the *Queen Mary*. The *Queen Mary* succeeded the *Mauritania* as the holder of the Atlantic Blue Riband. There was also a thriving trade in garden furniture made from the ships' timbers. The company ceased to operate in 1981.

The cable laying ship, *Sentinel*, waiting to be broken up at Hughes Bolkows in 1977.

Fishing

In 1880 there was a suggestion that a fish trade could be developed in the town, but the effort to establish this was a failure. Royal Assent was granted in June 1882 for the formation of a Harbour Commission which would play an important role in the development of the port and the harbour as well as the fishing industry. The year 1902 saw the first move to organise fishing from Blyth and make it a centre for the industry. The Harbour Commissioners had already provided useful facilities, but there was still two important aspects to consider:

    1. Landing of fish at Blyth by boat owners.
    2. Attracting the fish buyers.

The North East Railway Company granted special facilities for the trade and the Harbour Commissioners agreed to give every possible support.

The following years were a mixed bag of good and poor herring catches, but the Scottish 'fisher lasses' gutting and packing herring for export to Germany were a famous local sight.

One of the disadvantages to the town was the smell in the area of Wensleydale Terrace and the Links Road.

In 1910 the White Fish Industry was progressing and the Port of Blyth Steam Fishing and Ice Co. Limited was formed. A special train left the siding beside the fish dock everyday at 5.30 pm taking fish to York.

The Post of Blyth Fishing Co. was started in 1912 but the outbreak of the First World War in 1914 had a dramatic effect on the industry. The company's vessels were requisitioned by the government as were the fishing sheds and plots, the ice factory was dismantled, the machinery was sold and a submarine base established. After the war there was nothing to re-establish the herring or white fish trade as a major industry.

The *Lord Durham*, a steam ketch built at Middlesbrough in 1911, is a typical example of the boats which fished from Blyth. Steam screw powered, it was a trawler fishing with a crew of nine. Originally owned by the Port of Blyth Steam Fishing and Ice Co. Ltd, it was transferred to Grimsby and sold in August 1913. The *Lord Durham* was scrapped in Holland in 1937.

Prince Line Trawlers at Blyth Fish Quay, 1910. In January 1910, six Prince Line Trawlers were transferred on a time charter for the purpose of inaugurating a white fish market at Blyth. They were: *Welsh*, *Imperial*, *Scottish*, *Merchant*, *Egyptian* and *Grecian Prince*. *Merchant* and *Egyptian Prince* were both lost in August 1916.

The scene in 1999. The Fish Market buildings were demolished in October 1983 to make way for the Ro-Ro terminal, *Blyth Progress*, which came into use in 1984.

The Sceptre.

Bought by John Liddell of Blyth in 1945, *The Sceptre* spent twenty years at Blyth before moving to North Shields. Sold out of fishing in the early 1990s, she lay for some time in the Albert Edward Dock in North Shields. She was finally moved to Lemington where she was considerably altered for pleasure use.

Golden Days entering South Harbour. Built in 1949 for Robert Liddell, Harold Reed and Hugh Patterson, she worked out of Blyth for thirty-two years.

She finished her days in Fleetwood, being de-commissioned and broken up in 1996. However, it is possible that her remains are lying on Thornton Marsh, Fleetwood.

Harold Reed and Hugh Patterson working aboard the *Golden Days*.

Enterprise – built in Polruan, Cornwall in 1981. She came to Blyth in 1988 and was re-named *Homeland* belonging to Peter and Paul Dent of Newbiggin.

Shearbill – built at Fraserburgh in 1956 and owned by Roy Denton of Blyth.

The old fishing sheds in March 1988 before demolition. The shed on the left belonged to Lawrence Hedley but is thought to have originally been a canteen. Hugh Patterson's (on the right) was either an engineering or blacksmith's shed serving the fish quay.

Storage for fishermen's gear in 1999.

FIRE AND RESCUE

The Blyth LNER Swimming Club Lifeguard Team, 16th July 1961. They were
the winners of the Northumbria Trophy at the Northumberland and Durham
Lifeguard Competition. Back row: J. Rowell, J. Ward, P. Butters. Front row:
E. Armstrong, M. Patterson, N. Jackson. They were Blyth's first ever lifeguard
team.

In May 1961 the Blyth LNER Swimming Club established the first Lifeguard Team in Blyth. Six members took the test in the sea lasting nearly three hours. It involved fully clothed rescues; breaking strangleholds in the water; resuscitation techniques; reel and line; handling a boat and a final 800 metres swim.

Later in the same year the team held off the challenge of five other teams to win the Northumberland and Durham Lifeguard Trophy, the first time the contest had been held in the sea. In 1962 another six members passed the lifeguard sea test and the club began its exchange visits with the DLRG Lifeguard Club from Bremen in Germany.

Today the Blyth Lifeguard and Swimming Club has thirty-nine qualified lifeguards and six qualified beach lifesavers. Over the years the club has won a host of championships at local and national level and at all age groups. Club members provide a number of courses to encourage people to learn to swim and, if they want to, go on to improve their techniques by taking part in competitive swimming and ultimately go on to become lifeguards.

Now a lifeguard has to undergo a minimum of thirty-three hours training, learning a multitude of skills to equip them for today's rescues. These volunteers patrol an area from Blyth Harbour to St Mary's Island during the summer months and also provide lifeguards to cover swimming galas and parties at the Blyth Swimming Baths.

During the summer, lifeguard training takes place in the North Sea, which is cold at any time of the year. Locals and visitors can be assured that when the flag is flying at the Lifeguard Watch House near the promenade on the South Beach that a team of dedicated people are watching.

The Lifeguard Team, 20th February 1999. Back row: Adam Dixon, Stuart Dawson, Phillip Dawson. Front row: Becky Turton, Maureen Harrison, Michele Weedy.

In this, the 175th Anniversary year of the Royal National Lifeboat Institution, it seems only fitting that the Blyth lifeboats and their many courageous crews should be mentioned. This photograph, taken in the 1960s, shows the crew talking to the then Honorary Secretary, Captain H. Rowe (left). The crew members are John David Kerr, Bowman and holder of the RNLI Bronze Medal, the Maude Smith Award for the most courageous rescue at sea in 1962 and a Silver Medal from the King of Norway for saving life at sea, William Henry, James Skinner, James Skinner jnr, Thomas Fawcus, Coxswain and holder of the RNLI Silver Medal, Albert Cavener, Shore Watchman, and Sammy Crawford, 2nd Coxswain.

The crew of 1999, led, from left to right, by Coxswain David Innes, Edward Barnes, Kevin Barnes, Garry Moss (Mechanic), Matthew Coulson, Peter Morton, Graham Short and Stanley Marshall. Today's crews wear the most modern lifejackets and waterproof clothing available compared with the crews of the 1960s who wore thigh high boots, a long yellow oilskin, a souwester and a cork lifejacket.

Left: Joshua Wheatley, Coxswain of the Blyth Lifeboat from 1926 to 1949. Josh, as he was always known, was also the Coxswain of the Cambois Lifeboat from 1923 until 1926 when he was transferred to Blyth. At Cambois, the lifeboat was of the 'pulling' type. The boat was rowed out by the crews with their back to the sea with only the coxswain on the helm being able to see what was in front of them, thus the name 'pulling'. Coxswain Wheatley came to Blyth to take command of the *Joseph Adlam* motor lifeboat which remained on station until 1948 when it was replaced by the *Winston Churchill* lifeboat, a gift from the Civil Service Lifeboat Fund. Awarded the RNLI Bronze Medal in 1938 and the RNLI Thanks on Vellum in 1949, Coxswain Wheatley was often involved in rescues involving naval ships and aircraft during the war years.

Right: David Innes was appointed Coxswain of the *Windsor Runner* in 1998. He joined the crew in 1987 and has taken part in many rescues. His job differs from that of Coxswain Wheatley as on board his £1.4 million lifeboat he has the most modern equipment to aid in searches, whereas Coxswain Wheatley had to rely on his eyesight to find those in trouble. The *Windsor Runner* Lifeboat is fast and comfortable, the crew can stay in the dry, warm cabin until they reach their casualty whereas the previous crews had to brave the elements from launch. Modern technology enable the crews to keep in contact with the coastguard, the casualty and any other rescue services involved. The crews of the old lifeboats had to rely on signals from rockets on the shore or by Morse Code from Aldis lamps, and in later years early radio sets.

The opening day of the then new Fire Station in Union Street, 3rd September 1924, the Brigade having moved from the old station in Seaforth Street. It was decided to relocate to a site on Cowpen Road where access to the town was much easier. This station was officially opened on 28th April 1987.

The station is manned by four watches, Red, White, Blue and Green. Each Watch is made up of 12 men, one Sub-Officer, two Leading Fire Fighters and nine Fire Fighters. Each watch works a 42 hour week. Prior to 1979, the working hours were split into three watches, Green Watch was added to bring the number of hours down. Blyth is a two pump station and the current appliances are based on the Volvo FL6. 14 wagon chassis with Carmichael International bodyworks. They are composite appliances carrying both fire fighting and rescue equipment which includes hydraulic shears to cut people out of crashed vehicles and inflatable air bags capable of lifting 21 tons.

The first New Delaval Ambulance, 1912. The driver-nurse was Mrs Jane Thorne (née Hogarth). The man in the bowler hat was Mr R. Major. Some of the men in the first aid team were members of the Cotton and Smith families.

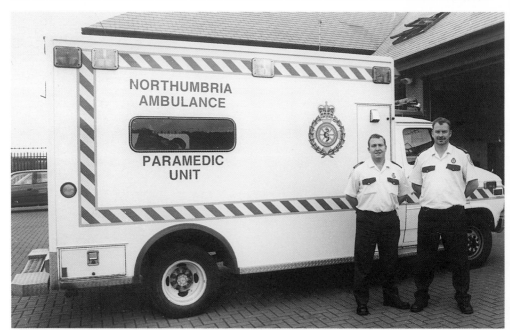

The ambulance of today is a far cry from the days of the stretcher and two blankets. The crew are no longer a driver and helper, but highly trained medics capable of saving lives before the arrival of a doctor. Pictured with the ambulance are Station Officer Paramedic Stephen Eke (left) and Ambulance Paramedic Bryan Hesp.

LEISURE AND SPORT

In June 1932 the Blyth Tennis Club on Plessey Road opened new hard courts. They were opened by Mrs T.W. Crozier and Mrs W.B. Parson. Others in the photograph include: Mrs Rutherford, Mrs J.T. Thompson of Hartford Hall, Miss M. Parson, Miss P. Armstrong, Ald Crozier, Mr Parsons, Mr C.G. Gallon and Mr W. Thompson.

Memories of the Beach and Promenade
by Eldred Routledge

The promenade was constructed during the depression of the 1920s when hundreds of men were looking for work. My father was one of them, he received the princely sum of thirty shillings (£1.50) 'dole' money.

In its heyday, the beach and promenade were very popular with the towns' people – a picnic on the sands was a treat. A penny for a pot of boiling water from the Jubilee Cafe and 'Bob's Your Uncle'.

The square tents belonged to the council, they could be hired for sixpence (two and a half pence) a day. A deck chair was three pence. The canvas covers were green. On summer nights people would go to the bandstand to be entertained by the Pierrots, they were a troupe of singers, dancers, musicians and a comedian called Harry Goodfellow. He performed the same act every night, told the same jokes, but we all laughed just the same.

Once a year the *Daily Mail* organised a sandcastle competition. This happened at low tide when the sand was still damp. The beach was marked off into two yard squares which was the area allowed to build our castles. There were prizes at the end of the day, but I cannot ever remember winning one.

During the 1920s and '30s, the beach between the piers was very popular, so much so that Seghini had a wooden hut on the sand from which ice cream and sweets could be bought.

Young men of the day would show off their prowess by diving from the top rail of the pier into the water below. There were no local swimming baths and pools then.

The bandstand was also the venue for Sunday night concerts by the local brass bands. The Cowpen and Crofton Collieries had a first class band, as did the London and North Eastern Railway.

Blyth beach in the 1930s.

The bandstand eventually fell into disrepair, the window panels were removed and the site was partially filled with water to form a paddling pool for children.

Many years later it was suggested that some money be spent on a facelift. A lady councillor (I cannot remember her name) stood up and said, 'That would be a waste of money. I don't suppose the 'thing' has ever been used.' She was either very young, or came from 'down south'!

The beach today is, I'm sad to say, not the place it used to be. How do I know, because I walk my dog there every morning. (Yes I do clean up after her as do most other responsible dog owners.) Seaweed apart, most of the debris on the high water mark is of human origin – plastic of all description, bottles, cans, fishermen's hooks and sinkers, also their empty bait bags. The beach cleaner runs along the high tide water mark about once a week and makes a very good job, but the next tide brings it all back.

As for the promenade the two big concrete shelters have been demolished and the once beautiful balustrade has almost disappeared. The chalets in which people took a great pride became targets for vandalism and graffiti and unfortunately the council could not maintain the cost of repairs.

Most of the dunes on the beach have long since disappeared. Sand extraction being the main culprit. Contractors, one at Blyth and another at Seaton Sluice, started loading sand from the beach using horses and carts with men filling them using shovels. As the demand for sand increased, the carts became lorries and the hand filling by men was replaced by mechanical shovels. Many thousands of tons per year being removed before the council realised that the natural forces production system could not keep up with man's greed. Sand extraction was eventually stopped but sadly the beaches have never recovered.

The beach in 1999.

Ridley Park Bandstand in 1920. The bandstand was a summer time rendezvous to listen to the brass bands playing on a Sunday night. The putting green nearby was also an attraction, the fee was an old penny per round.

Today, the site is now occupied by a Rose Garden. The construction was assisted financially by Blyth Round Table and opened in 1970.

Ridley Park Lake, *circa* 1930. The lake in the park was very popular at this time. Boys would sail their model yachts and motor boats. However, the fountain in the middle proved a hazard when socks and shoes had to be discarded to retrieve a boat caught fast in the middle.

The paddling pool today. The park is still very popular and the children's play areas are in use all the year round. There are amenities for all ages – swings, slides and roundabouts and of course the 'Ridley' and 'Excelsior' bowling greens.

Blyth Cricket Team, 1960.
Back row: B. Simpson,
J. Harland, M. Oldfield,
F. Rockett, J. Prior,
M. Bruce. Front row:
G. Heatley, W. Emery,
C. Pearson (captain),
N. Mitcheson, A. Harper.
Blyth Cricket Club was
formed at a meeting on
5th June 1883. Some of
the people at that meeting
had names synonymous to
Blyth, such as: Nelson,
Saunders, Manners,
Robinson, Charlton, Hope,
Towers, Soulsby, Parsons,
Routledge and Heatley.
The Revd W. Maddison

was elected chairman, R.R. Wallace elected treasurer and J.B. Nelson elected
secretary. The subscriptions were to be ten shillings and six pence (53 pence)
and the club was called the 'Blyth District Cricket Club'. Their playing field,
which belonged to the Harbour Commission, was near Blagdon Terrace. After
years of being in and out of the doldrums, the club found a new home on
Plessey Road in 1924. For the first time in the club's history, Blyth won the
league in 1958. Success was due to the emergence of local lads like Jack
Chicken, Cecil Pearson, Graeme Heatley, Neil Mitcheson and brothers Harry
and Brian Davis – their talents all coming together at the same time. In 1974,
Blyth Cricket and Tennis Club amalgamated with Blyth Rugby Club. This has
proved to be a financial success. Everyone hopes that success on the playing
fields will follow.

Blyth Cricket Team, 1998. Back row: S. Spoljaric, A.E. Routledge,
C. Spence, M. Hughes, K. Sadler, N. Humble, T. Etherington. Front
row: I. Anderson, N. Melling, J. Purvis, P. Cormack, S. Singh.

Blyth Spartans

Blyth Spartans Football Club is perhaps best remembered for their outstanding FA Cup run in the 1970s, but the club has a very long and proud history prior to that time.

The old Blyth Football Club, which joined the Northern Alliance in 1892 and carried on for seven years playing their games at the Blagdon Terrace Ground, were the first professional team to play in Blyth.

The Spartans were founded in 1899 under the title of Blyth Spartans Athletic Club and began in affiliated football in September 1901 as members of the Northumberland League.

Their FA Cup ambitions go back to the 1922-23 season, the first time they reached the first round proper, when they were defeated by Stoke City 3-0. Croft Park has not always been the home of the Spartans. The first ground was near to Percy's Gardens which were at the junction of Middleton Street and Cypress Gardens.

After that they were at 'Spion Kop' (adjoining the North, later Bates Pit) from September 1901 to the end of the 1904-05 season. They then moved to Plessey Road (opposite Croft Park) for a season before moving to Thornton Cottage for the start of the 1906-07 season. Croft Park was officially opened in 1909, the ground belonging to the Thoroton and Croft Trustees, and the team has played there ever since.

The style of the strip may have changed over the years but the team has always played in green and white stripes.

Blyth Spartans, *circa* 1912.

Giant Killers

There can be few people living in Blyth who have not heard of the FA Cup exploits of the Spartans. The memorable replay against Wrexham at St James' Park in 1978 was reported the world over. Television crews followed the part-timers to work and thousands of words were written by top sports writers of how this almost unknown team from South East Northumberland, that played in the Northern League, had knocked out top flight opposition in fairy tale style to reach the fifth round proper of the most famous cup competition in the world.

It all started with a 3-0 victory over fellow Northern League outfit Shildon in the first qualifying round back in September 1977. Next it was another Northern League side, Crook Town, who fell victims to Spartans but this time only after a replay at Croft Park – once again the score was 3-0. In the third qualifying round, Consett, again a Northern League side were defeated in a 4-1 victory. The fourth qualifying round proved to be a little more difficult. This time top Northern League side Bishop Auckland were the opposition but Blyth pulled off a 1-0 victory.

Tension was mounting in the Blyth camp as the next round, the first round proper, meant that the clubs from the lower divisions of the Football League were included in the draw. Blyth got a home draw against Burscough, from the North West Combination. But once again the Spartans showed that they were a top squad sending the visitors home disappointed with an Ian Mutrie goal putting Blyth through to the next round.

By now the town was beginning to get a touch of cup fever. Fans and town's people alike gathered around radios to hear the draw for the next round. Again Blyth gained a home tie – against Chesterfield from the Third Division, managed by Arthur Cox who later went on to manage Newcastle.

The visitors brought a considerable following with them to Croft Park and the ground was full to capacity with an atmosphere that only a cup game brings. Striker Stephen Jones eventually produced the goods that sent the opposition home with their tails between their legs.

Right: The programme from Blyth Spartans' FA Cup replay against Wrexham at St James' Park in 1978. Left to right: Dave Clarke, Ron Guthrie and Terry Johnson.

By now cup fever was beginning to take hold and the big question was, 'Who would be next?' The local Special Constabulary were put on standby for crowd control duties and plans were being drawn up to make arrangements for parking for visitors close to the ground.

Once again Blyth gained a home draw, this time against Enfield Town from the Isthmian League. The question on everyone's lips was, 'When will a First or Second Division side come to Blyth?'

A capacity crowd at Croft Park, that could be heard all over the town, saw the Spartans produce an outstanding performance to send them marching on into the next round. This time it was pitman Alan Shoulder, who later went on to play for Newcastle, who scored the vital goal. Blyth were in the fourth round.

Now everyone wanted to know who Blyth Spartans were. Who were these part-timers who could play top class football and achieve stardom almost overnight? What made them and their mentors tick? The quest for information was on, any loyal supporter could answer the questions but the rags to riches story had to be written in a particular style.

The manager and striker was Brian Slane, a maths teacher from County Durham who had joined the club nine years previously. He had taken part in superb but not so momentous cup runs in '71 and '74, when both times Blyth went out to League opposition.

Their coach was a vociferous bow-legged mechanical engineer called Jack Marks, whose heart was in football and his relationship with Slane meant the two were often referred to as the Clough and Taylor of non-league football. Their ability to motivate players and to survey their opposition was second to non. Marks was often hoarse after a game, due to him shouting encouragement and instructions to his team.

Terry Johnson at his fruit and veg stall in Blyth Market, April 1999.

The Spartans' squad included a number of players that had league experience. Their knowledge and experience helped the younger members of the squad and in general stabilised the team. Goalkeeper, Dave Clark, often had to dig deep into his experiences as a Newcastle United player to keep the opposition at bay. He was ably supported by another former Newcastle player, Ron Guthrie who had won a cup winners medal with Sunderland.

A midfield trio of Eddie Alder, Michael Dagless and Terry Johnson could also be relied upon, and more often than enough one of them got their names on the score sheet. Alder, an England Amateur international player, had played for the Spartans for 12 seasons. Dagless, an England Youth International and English Universities player, was like his manager a school teacher. Johnson was a player with a pedigree; for two seasons he was top scorer at Brentford and had previously played at Newcastle and Southend.

This is only a selection of the squad that the Spartans used for their cup run. They were the players that often grabbed the headlines, however, it was the squad's efforts that made the Spartans mighty.

Blyth's quality squad was in no small way due to the tireless work of chairman Jimmy Turney, who scoured grounds looking for players to recommend and then sign for Spartans. Jimmy, a local builder from nearby Seaton Sluice, was a former player who hung up his boots and joined the board.

The players remained level headed throughout the campaign, speaking with the press and posing for photographs at every opportunity but never getting big headed.

Once again it was draw day and everyone waited with baited breath. The whole town was silent as the draw was made. Blyth got an away tie at Stoke City, a Second Division club with a proud cup history. As the draw was made, miners working two miles out under the North Sea were informed by the pit's control room.

The town exploded into a sea of Green and White, just about everyone wore the Spartans' colours. Ticket allocation meant that only the lucky ones could go to Stoke for the game and the supporters' club arranged transport to the Potteries.

Saturday dawned cold and very, very wet. The team were already in Stoke and the majority of supporters had left Blyth only to find out that the game had been called off an hour before the kick-off. The game had to be played the following week.

People gathered around radios and television to hear snippets of news from the game which Blyth eventually won 3-2 with goals from Terry Johnson (2) and Steve Carney. Stoke's goals were scored by Garth Crooks and Viv Busby. The town went mad that night with supporters waiting for the team bus to return and the jubilant Spartans were given a hero's reception.

Secretary, George Watson had been preparing for a replay not at Croft Park but at St James' Park as he knew the whole town would want to see that game, but the deed had been done away from home.

The draw was made, and Blyth were away again, this time to Wrexham who had beaten Newcastle 4-1 in the previous round. Eight thousand tickets were allocated to Blyth fans at the Racecourse ground. For a town with a population of just under 36,000 there were going to be a lot of disappointed people.

Once again radios and televisions provided the link to the game, the normally busy market was almost deserted and staff in shops were in silent groups around radios awaiting news. Blyth were in the lead for much of the game and everyone was praying for the referees whistle to blow but Dixie

McNeil pulled one back for Wrexham. The disputed corner kick the goal came from is still a talking point today.

So a replay loomed with the victors looking forward to facing Arsenal. The replay was arranged for 27th February 1978 at St James' Park.

By mid afternoon, Blyth had begun to empty, every bus bound for Newcastle was full of Spartans fans and by six o'clock the town was almost empty with everyone wanting to be at the game – in fact 43,000, most from Blyth, filled St James.

One local wit had predicted the score on a sign post into Blyth. On a sign which normally read BLYTH 2 and underneath NEWSHAM 1, the wit had changed the Newsham into Wrexham but alas it was not to be.

Wrexham took the lead with a penalty from Whittle and then that man McNeil made it 2-0 before the break. Blyth came out for the second half determined and a Terry Johnson goal rocked Wrexham and St James' roared. However, despite several valiant efforts Wrexham held on and made it to the next round.

The then secretary of the Football League, Ted Crocker, wrote, 'Blyth Spartans are the most famous non-League side in the country.'

Blyth Spartans on the day of the final of the Northumberland Senior Cup held at St James' Park, 2nd May 1998. Back row: Kona Hislop, Tony Kennedy, Willie Moat, Anth Cole, Martin Pike, John Gamble, Stephen Dann, Stephen Jones, Willie Wilson, Glen Martin, John Burridge. Front row: Jon Atkinson, Steven Walker, Michael Farrey, Joe Rose (mascot), Andrew Dodds (mascot), Glen Renforth, Kevin McGarigele, John Tinkler. The Spartans were beaten 2-0 by Bedlington.

Blyth Rugby Football Club, 1922-23. Included in the back row: T. Nicholson, J. Bowden, W. Robinson, W. Morrision, R. Johnson, C. Atkinson, H. Norman, F. Nicholson, B. Bowman, G. Watson. Front row: F. Bailey, E. Eadington, J. Watson, N. Jackson, S. Armstrong, V. Straker, J. Morrison. Blyth RFC was founded in 1921 by Norman Jackson. The team played their first game against Seghill, on 26th September 1921, which they won 20 points to nil. However, in 1923 due to financial difficulties, amongst other things, the club ceased to operate. In 1961, Bernie Cranmer senior banded together a group of men and reformed Blyth RFC. The first captain of the newly formed club was G. Heatley. They played their games on pitches at the Plessey Road Ground and at council owned pitches at Cowpen and Gloucester lodge. The club secured the use of the Cricket Club bar in 1967 and they amalgamated with the Cricket Club in 1971. One former Blyth player, George Newstead, became secretary of the West Australian Rugby Union in 1950 and was awarded an MBE in 1975.

Blyth Buccaneers, 1998-99. Back row: Jason Newall, Tony Armstrong, John Hayes, Dave Walker, Alan Patterson, Paul Charlton, Mel Cole, Cliff Charlton, Jason Miller. Front row: Ian Coundon, Dennis Wilson, Jimmy Smith, Joe Miller, Brian Rees, Allan Stewart, Clem Ferguson.

PUBS AND CLUBS

The Golden Fleece, 1999. A panoramic view of the river can be seen from this pub, having been built on the shoreline. In recent years a conservatory type lounge has been added to the front of the building improving the view. Being so close to the river, however, has its disadvantages. When a Spring Tide, heavy rainfall and high winds coincide, the results can be disastrous. On many occasions a fire tender has been called to pump out the flooded cellar.

Pubs and Clubs

In the 1950s and '60s there were 40 public houses and 17 clubs flourishing in the town. The workers in the heavy industries of mining, shipbuilding and shipbreaking as well as visiting seamen kept the 'tills ringing'.

As the industrial life of Blyth dwindled and ceased, many public houses had to close their doors. Some were demolished, while others became banks, building societies, shops and in one instance a bingo hall.

New public houses have been built in areas of new housing developments. These include: The Spartan Hotel, 12th Avenue in 1973, The Sea Horse, Plessey Road in 1965, The Isabella, Southend Avenue in 1973, The Golden Eagle, Albion Way in 1974 – for one year it was called Ye Olde England – and The South Beach in 1977. The Gwentland Hotel in Wensleydale Terrace changed its name to the Ridley Park Hotel in 1979 when it gained its first liquor licence.

The Social and Workingmen's Clubs are patronised mainly by older residents on a membership basis. Drinks are usually cheaper than in public houses. Ladies in the bar are still looked upon askance in some clubs.

With the demise of youth clubs and dance halls, the pubs have become the gathering places of the young. The character of most has changed over the two decades. Meals, live entertainment, bingo, quizzes, large screen cable or satellite television, slot machines etc, are all enticements to the public.

This building was once The Ship public house in Albert Street and faced the shipyard gates. When this photograph was taken it was known as the Plessey Sports Club. There is a possibility that this building was originally used for religious services, but this has not been confirmed.

The Comrades' Club. This photograph was taken in 1919 when the first Comrades Club was started in this building in Sussex Street. The property was the former Black Bull Inn which had closed as a public house in 1918. The club later moved to the rooms in High Street before moving to a more permanent site in the old school in Cowpen Colliery. The man standing sixth from the left is Charles Robert Kinghorn, the soldier is Jack Roach.

The club today. During 1958 the present club was built in Wright Street, the old club was demolished with the rest of Cowpen Colliery. In 1970 the name was changed from Cowpen and Newsham Comrades' Club to Blyth Comrades' Club.

The Market Hotel was opened in Market Street before 1873 and was closed in 1982. The 'Market' was one of the town centre pubs which closed due to lack of customers. Others which closed for the same reason include: The Globe, The White Swan, The Station Hotel and The Commercial Inn. The 'Market' has become a frozen food shop (below). The character of the building has been lost by the unsympathetic replacement of the ground floor frontage and the removal of the dormer windows.

Joiners' Arms, Coomassie Road. The houses in Wood Street and Crofton Street were demolished in the mid 1960s. The house next to the pub was also knocked down about the same time. The council built blocks of flats on the land.

The Joiners' Arms today.

The Travellers' Rest, Regent Street. The pub was opened before 1873, rebuilt in 1897 and demolished in September 1998. It was originally one of the finest buildings in Blyth but never achieved its full potential as a hotel. After a chequered career, and standing derelict for several years, it was finally demolished in 1998.

Below: Demolition in progress.

The Commercial Inn in Regent Street was closed in 1973 and is now the Northern Rock Building Society. It is situated between Burton's and the entrance to the Keelrow Shopping Mall. Two very attractive doorways have been lost to 'modernisation'.

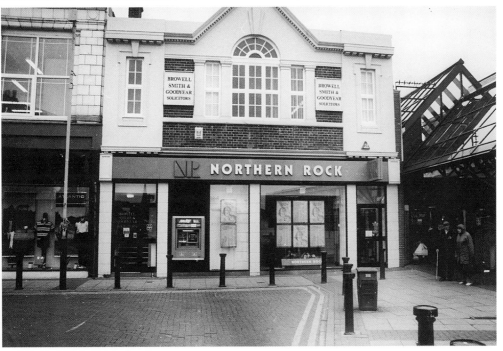

The Pineapple Inn, Regent Street/Bowes Street corner.

The pub was closed in 1973 and is now a branch of the National Westminster Bank.

The Croft, Regent Street. The name of the pub was changed to The Porthole in 1974. In 1996 the name was changed again to 'Joe Cavner's' after the owner's late father.

Cowpen Colliery Inn, Marlow Street, with the Miners' Arms next door. The stone steps and iron handrail were part of the foot bridge which spanned the Blyth to Newsham railway line. Crossing the bridge at this point led to the rows of houses in the mining community of Cowpen Colliery. These houses and the colliery workshops were demolished and the site cleared in the early 1960s. The Leisure Centre and Bolam Avenue now occupy this area. The small building behind the Cowpen Colliery Inn was the Miners' Arms which opened before 1873 and closed in 1937.

The Top House, Marlow Street, today. The Cowpen Colliery Inn was always referred to as the 'Top House' hence the name change.

The Seven Stars public house was opened before 1822 and closed in 1967. It was very popular with seamen waiting for their ships to be loaded with cargoes of coal from the staithes on the north side of the river. At the demise of the coal industry the number of customers was so reduced it resulted in its closure. In 1992 the Wind Farm Generators were built for the Blyth Harbour Commissioners. Eight of the windmills were erected on the North Pier, the ninth stands on the site by the Seven Stars (left). The Harbour Commissioners are planning to build at least one more generator which will be sited off-shore.

The Black Diamond, Newsham, in the late 1940s.

The scene in 1999.

The Bebside Inn, Bebside Front Street, *circa* 1900.

Bebside Front Street, 1998. The row of houses in Front Street were known locally as 'The Black and White Cottages'. The houses, signal box and railway crossing gates have all gone. There is now a pole barrier on the rail crossing.

The Three Horse Shoes, Horton, 1910.

The Shoes, 1998.

Acknowledgements

The authors would like to thank:

J. Allen, W. Allen, M. Bagley, R. Balmer, J. Beamish, G. Bell, the Revd B. Benison, Blyth Harbour Commission, Blyth Local History Society, R.C. Bush, R. Chicken, R. Cottrill, G. Cozens, L. Davison, A. Donnelly, J. Evans, M. Harrison, D. Hetherington, J. Kennedy, Fr. J. Lennox, A. Madgwick, W. Mann, J. Morgan, Newcastle Libraries and Information Services, S. Parker, H. Patterson, the Revd R. Pringle, L. Richardson, M. Roach, H. Robson, C. Rockett, Royal Northumberland Yacht Club, C. Smith, J. Soulsby, M. Speight, F. Stannard, C. Taylor, J. & J. Tuttiett, J. Watson, C. White, E. Whiteman, A. Wilkinson, H. Garrod, W. Robson.

Newcastle Libraries and Information Services Photographs

Pages: 44T, 117T, 122T, 124T.

Septimus Mole (centre) and his staff in the early days of their cycle business in Regent Street.

George Hailes, better known as 'Black Geordie' was a local character well-known around the harbour and dock area. He was born in South Shields in 1874 and moved to Blyth when he was 12. He lived in an old stable near Blyth Cemetery at South Beach. It is said that the Great Coat he is wearing belonged to the late Colonel Wright of Wrights timber company. For many years this photograph hung in the office of Alan Wilkinson a director of that company. Black Geordie was not without friends in the town for during service in the First World War, food parcels were sent to him by the local police on behalf of the town's people as it was known he had no relatives. George died in Preston Hospital, North Shields, aged 73 in 1947.

The People's History

To find out more about this unique series of local history books – and to receive a catalogue of the latest titles – send a large stamped addressed envelope to:

The People's History Ltd
Suite 1
Byron House
Seaham Grange Business Park
Seaham
County Durham
SR7 0PY